FOX
IN YOUR GARDEN

DOREEN KING

Photographs: Doreen and Michael King

t.f.h.
KINGDOM

CONTENTS

t.f.h.
KINGDOM

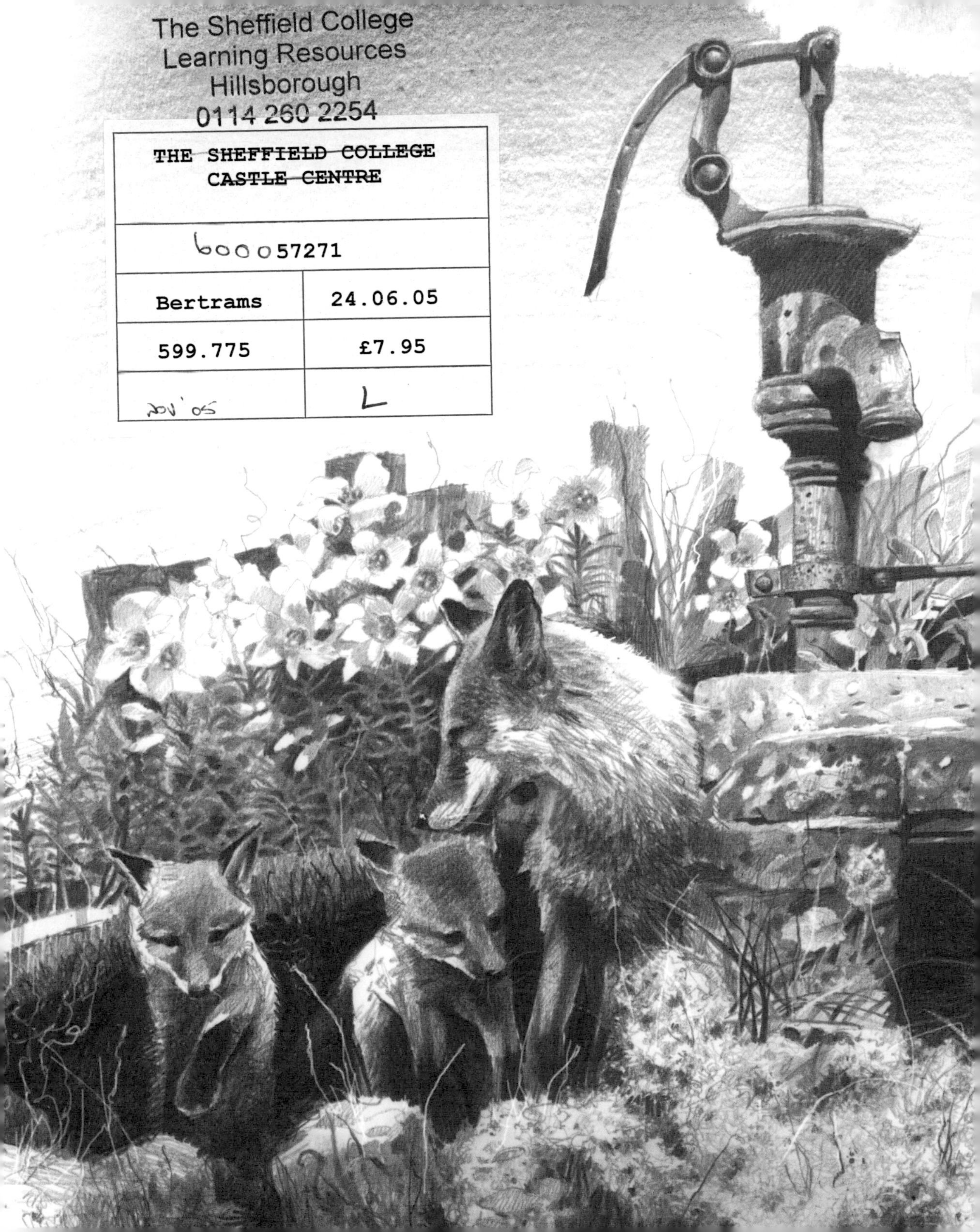

CHAPTER 1

Introducing the FOX

The Red Fox: one of the largest wild carnivores in Britain.

The Red Fox is a traditional representative of British wildlife. It is one of our largest wild carnivores, very closely related to the domestic dog. As it shares many of the characteristics of the pet dog it can also attract a certain amount of understanding, sympathy and respect.

So closely was the Red Fox linked to the British countryside in the past that it was sometimes said that, as long as the Red Fox was there, there was some countryside left in Great Britain. However, changes in farming and modern living have forced foxes to adapt, often moving into towns and suburbs. Nowadays, most people are likely to have seen the modern urban fox at one time or another.

Since the Red Fox is the only fox to be found in the British Isles, it is simply called 'the fox' in this book except where it is necessary to distinguish between species.

Predators

The fox has been persecuted for many, many years, both by farmers and sportsmen and, more generally, in an attempt to eradicate rabies. Nevertheless, the fascination exerted by the fox has meant that it has also been held in some reverence. Indeed, foxes were imported into Great Britain during the 19th century – with the purpose of maintaining a high population to satisfy the popular sport of fox hunting.

In Great Britain in the past, and in some parts of the world today, foxes have been used as a valuable food commodity. In this country today they are hunted mainly for sport, and very occasionally for fur. They used to be hunted for fur from about October to February, the fur being used mainly for coat trimmings, as British fox fur was not of sufficiently high quality for coats and stoles. They were taken by trapping or by digging out with terriers and clubbing. They were also sometimes caught by lurchers (large, cross-bred dogs). However, although real fur trimmings were still moderately fashionable in the 1960s, pressure from environmental groups and education have brought about the almost exclusive use of synthetic fur for this purpose today. The fox is still hunted – but for sport rather than for food or fur.

CHAPTER 1

The Fox in Folklore

Like all larger-than-life characters, the fox has had many legends grow up around it over the years. For instance, foxes are sometimes depicted as carrying large prey over their shoulders. Needless to say, they don't – they drag it. Foxes have also been associated with grapes in folklore. They do love grapes, they eat any they can get, ripe and unripe, not confining themselves to the ripe ones, as is claimed in the old tales.

Another story about the fox deals with parasite eradication. It is said that the fox will take a twig in its mouth and back into a pond. Its fleas then jump onto the twig as the fox backs into the water, whereupon the fox releases the twig with the fleas on it. While it must be said that the fox does not have the same degree of access to flea medications as the domestic dog, this story sounds a little far-fetched, to say the least!

Again according to legend, the fox catches hedgehogs by urinating upon the unfortunate creatures until they uncurl from their balls. Foxes do indeed take hedgehogs, but they do so by attacking their accessible parts – usually the head and legs if the hedgehog is slow to curl up. Young or sickly hedgehogs are the usual victims.

Over the years, people have attributed various human characteristics to the fox. As far back as 500 BC, when Aesop wrote his famous fables, the fox was depicted as being clever. A 12th century French poem called *Reynard the Fox* (basically a satire about the shortcomings of society in which people are represented by various beasts) is set in the court of King Noble, the lion. The other animals, led by Isengrim the wolf, complain to the King about Reynard, who is put on trial. He argues his way out of the charges charmingly and persuasively and promises to be good. Eventually, he is pardoned by the King – and proceeds to take his revenge on the wolf.

The fox is so much a part of our heritage that it has found its way into our language in such expressions as *As red as a fox*, *As cunning as a fox* and *As sly as a fox*. It has been credited with a very devious nature and with the intelligence to plan its hunting activity methodically.

Perhaps the fox is not quite as brilliant as legends would have us believe, but it really is a reasonably intelligent mammal – to the extent that hunters like to pursue it because it presents them with a reasonable challenge. That it has managed to survive for such a long period of time speaks for itself. What's more, it now seems likely that the fox will even survive the disappearance of traditional countryside quite well.

The cunning of the fox is celebrated in many songs and stories, including Aesop's fables.

CHAPTER 1

Foxes feel at home in suburban gardens.

The fox has given its name to an assortment of plants and phenomena:

- The Foxglove (*Digitalis purpurea*) is a well-known plant, and Digitalis from the flowers is extremely important for the treatment of heart diseases. Whether the plant was named because the flowers fit onto the feet of foxes is debatable.
- Fox bane (*Aconitum vulparia*) is a poisonous plant. The poison from its roots can be ground and at one time it was used to kill foxes.
- Fox sedge (*Carex vulpina*) might be so called because of its reddish flower.
- Foxing is the term given to the reddish-brown stains that appear on the pages of old books that have become damp.

Foxes into Suburbia

During the second half of the 20th century there has been a noticeable increase in the number of fox sightings in the centres of towns and cities. Here in Havering, on the eastern outskirts of London, there has been a remarkable change in the pattern of fox behaviour over the period 1986–1996. I receive many calls about wildlife every year and, during this 10-year period, the number of calls about garden foxes has increased dramatically. Their adaptation to garden life can be seen as a quest for survival amid the destruction of hedgerows, woods and fields, together with urban sprawl. Traditionally, hedgerows have been

Foxes especially enjoy untended corners of gardens.

used by a wide variety of wildlife and the destruction of hedgerows all over Essex during 1986–1996 is thought to be a major factor in the movement of foxes into gardens.

Foxes were common in the suburbs of London even in the 1940s, but now they have also adapted to living in the heart of London. However, they still prefer the suburbs, particularly areas that have a large proportion of properties with medium-sized gardens. The owners of such gardens usually buy sheds and plant a few hedges, and they may also have bird tables and large compost heaps – all of which are treasured by foxes. The density could be as high as two urban fox families for every square kilometre, and this could even rise to as high as five in some areas.

A description of the FOX

The Red Fox (*Vulpes vulpes*) that is present in Britain can also be seen in mainland Europe, Asia, Africa and America, as well as Australia. Its main distribution is from central Asia to the Siberian tundra.

Its Place in the Animal Kingdom

According to the Binomial System of Nomenclature, developed by the Swedish naturalist Carolus Linnaeus in the 18th century, living creatures and plants are divided into **Classes**, one of which groups together creatures that suckle their young and is known as **Mammalia**, or **Mammals**. Classes are then subdivided into **Orders**, and among the mammals are such orders as **Carnivora** or **Carnivores** (meat-eaters, for example, cats and dogs) and **Primates** (so-called 'highest' or 'prime' order, including monkeys, apes and man). The order Carnivora is then subdivided into **Families**. Foxes are found in the **Canidae** family, along with domestic dogs, wolves and dingoes. Canidae (canids) have four obvious canine teeth, which are used for killing and tearing. The shearing (carnassial) teeth are located in the sides of the mouth. Most species of canid have five toes on the forefeet and four on the hind. The fifth toe (or dew claw) on the forefoot is located on the inside of the leg, just above the foot.

Various Species

In its turn the canidae family is divided into various **Genera** (singular: *genus*), and foxes belong to the genera *Vulpes*, *Alopex*, *Otocyon* and *Fennecus*. There are only about 10 different species of foxes; the figure is not exact because there is always some debate about what

Arctic Fox.

constitutes a strain or variety and what constitutes an individual species. The Red Fox is the largest species, while the smallest is the Fennec Fox from North America. Others include the Arctic Fox, the Bat-eared Fox, and the American Grey (or Gray) Fox.

Bat-eared Foxes (*Otocyon* sp) eat insects and are not really carnivorous. Their ears act as heat exchangers, having a large surface area to help to control the body heat. Fennec Foxes (*Fennecus zerata*) also eat many insects, as well as small mammals. The Grey Fox (*Urocyon cinereoargenteus*) is arboreal (likes to spend most of its time in trees) and is hunted for its fur.

Grey (or Gray) Fox.

To return to our native fox: the Red Fox (*Vulpes vulpes*) has a red-brown coat and paler abdomen (often whitish), and there is usually a line of darker fur along its back. The backs of the ears are black, as are the fronts of the feet. The tail is often called the *brush*, and it sometimes has a white tip. There are colour varieties, among them the Silver Fox, which has a black coat with white tips to the long guard hairs, and the Cross Fox, which has the usual colour pattern with the addition of a black line down its back, bisected by another across its shoulders. All-white foxes and foxes with white patches have also been recorded.

Bat-eared Fox.

Distribution and Urbanisation

Red Foxes were introduced into the United States of America in the early 18th century and into Australia during the late 19th century. In the United States another member of the Canidae family, the Coyote, has adapted to city life. This is a larger animal, and it is potentially quite dangerous. Another American mammal that likes to take advantage of living close to humans is the North American Racoon (*Procyon lotor*), which is about twice the weight of the average Red Fox. Racoons are very probably the ancestors of canids. Red Foxes are found in many cities in Europe and in other parts of the world.

Fennec Fox.

This fox is accustomed to man,
but still keeps a wary eye open.

Surviving Against the Odds

In Great Britain, large predators such as bears and wolves disappeared a long time ago. Because of man's need to farm, foxes might also have disappeared were it not for the popularity of fox hunting. The fox is not generally considered a dangerous animal. There was a report in 1996 of a fox attacking a baby in a pram but, to my knowledge, this is the only report of such an incident occurring here. On the other hand, every year there are reports of pet dogs attacking children. The other potential danger to people is the spread of rabies, but fortunately this is not a problem in the British Isles at present.

Physical Characteristics

The average weight of the fox is 6.5–7kg (14–15lb) for the male (dog fox) and 5–5.5kg (11–12lb) for the female (vixen), which is comparable to the weight of a very large pet cat. The dog fox has an average head and body length of about 67cm (26in) and a tail of about 40cm (15$\frac{1}{2}$in), while the vixen has a head and body length of about 63cm (25in) and a tail of about 39cm (15in). Foxes living in the north of England tend to be slightly larger than those in the south.

In general, foxes are lean animals. They often look very scruffy in the summer, and I often receive calls from people who confuse this appearance with mange or starvation. At this time of year they shed their luxuriant, long guard hairs, and the thinner coat and sometimes practically hairless tail cause concern. This makes them rather appealing and favours them, as they tend to be fed rather well by caring people! This moult can last for several months, in fact for most of the spring and summer. During the autumn the coat becomes thicker and the longer guard hairs (about 5cm or 2in long) come back, making the fox look much fatter and healthier. Foxes seen at this time look about twice as fat as they do in summer, but of course food is actually much more plentiful in summer than in winter.

Foxes can sprint, reaching speeds of up to 60 kilometres per hour, but they can only sustain such a speed for a short time. They usually catch their prey by pouncing on it and dispatching it with a bite.

A fox's eyesight is somewhat different from that of a human. While foxes have good vision in dim light, they do not have our range of colour vision and they can see best at short range. Movement is detected very quickly, but a person standing still in full view is often unseen. To augment their night vision foxes have a special layer of cells (*tapetum lucidum*) which reflects the light back through the eye. Consequently, the light passes through the eye twice, increasing visual sensitivity. The eyes glow green at night because of this and the pupils form slits, similar to those of cats' eyes. Foxes also have sharp ears and keen noses.

The adaptable eyes and sharp ears of the fox. Note the dark backs of the ears.

A fox has 42 teeth, and it is the teeth that can give away the secret of its age – in life and death. If the chance arrives to examine a live fox closely, an estimate of its age can be made by examining how worn its teeth are, wear and tear being particularly noticeable on the incisors. A dead fox's teeth can be examined more closely to determine the age from the number of *year rings* on the teeth. Each winter a ring appears close to the root of each tooth – a layer of cemetum formed before the spring. The tooth can be soaked in a weak solution of nitric acid to remove the calcium, and thin sections of tooth can be cut and stained so that the rings show up under a microscope and can be counted.

Behaviour Patterns

Some foxes spend the day sleeping outside towns and cities, moving in at night to hunt for food. However, as I have already said, many have now moved into suburban gardens. They can be heard calling to each other at any time during the year – their high-pitched bark is similar to that of a small dog. However, during the mating season vixens let out high-pitched, harrowing, long-lasting screams that echo through the night. If the vixen is in a street, everyone living in the street is likely to

A 'singing' fox.

be awakened by her screams, which are usually answered very quickly by a dog fox. Abandoned cubs and adult foxes who have lost a partner may call all night long in vain.

Country foxes are said to live in family groups of one dog fox, a dominant vixen and several other vixens. However, in Havering all the foxes we have encountered are in a family of one pair and the annual offspring. Indeed, it is common to find one partner struggling to raise a family when the other has died. There is a long period of parental care and, during this time, the young learn their social and hunting skills. Foxes are also said to hunt in pairs or families (a group is called a *skulk*). Again, my observations in Havering are different – I usually see foxes hunting alone, and it is because they hunt alone that they sometimes need to call out.

Each fox has a pair of anal glands, and small scent glands on its feet and on its tail (brush). Like domestic dogs, foxes scent-mark their territories. Urine and faeces are used to communicate and record their presence. Usually vixens squat to urinate while the dog fox, like the male domestic dog, cocks his leg, but some dog foxes always squat.

In general, foxes communicate in a similar way to pet dogs, arching their backs, snarling and baring their teeth. Like dogs and cats, they make their hair stand on end when they are threatened to make themselves appear bigger and more formidable. When greeting family members they wag their tails. They also whine, squeak, yelp, bark and scream. The fox's scream, described earlier, has often been reported to the police by people who thought murder was being committed. Like domestic dogs, foxes love playing with old shoes, and old shoes scattered around the garden give a good indication that foxes play there.

Although most active at night foxes can often be seen during the day, particularly in summer. They like to sunbathe and sleep on shed roofs and in the middle of lawns if not disturbed. However, they are seen most frequently during the evening and also in late summer afternoons, when the juveniles come out to play close to their dens.

Lifespan and Mortality Rates

Captive foxes can live for 14 years or more – in fact, as long as pet dogs. However, wild foxes may only live for one to two years. About 50% of juvenile foxes are killed by cars, and up to 25% of urban juveniles are deliberately killed by snares, poison or injuries that lead to subsequent death; for instance, having been shot with an air rifle or a children's toy bow and arrow. A further 20% may die from various diseases. Winter lung infection is common, as is mange. A few more die as a result of fighting with other foxes and dogs. Autumn and winter fights are common among dog foxes, and vixens may die in summer fights at territory margins when they have young cubs to guard.

As I have said, foxes breed annually. It follows that, if there are four cubs in a litter then, if more than two survive, the fox population is increasing.

Like dogs, foxes enjoy a good stretch.

During the summer, a fox enjoys a quick nap on the lawn.

Range

Radio tracking (radio-telemetry) is the usual method for monitoring fox activity. The fox is caught and a radio transmitter is fitted to a collar or harness to be worn by the fox. When the fox is released, the signal from the collar is picked up by an aerial receiver, recording the fox's whereabouts. If different frequencies are used, several foxes can be monitored at once. With suitable batteries, the transmitters remain active for about two years.

Food for the FOX

The Fox's Diet

Urban foxes are usually quite self-sufficient when it comes to food, generally finding plenty to satisfy their appetites except in very bad weather or when they are ill. Perhaps it is surprising to hear that earthworms form a large part of this dedicated hunter's diet. Lawns may well be used for sunbathing during the day and for hunting worms at night!

Foxes are typical medium-sized carnivores and, as the word suggests, they live predominantly on meat. However, they eat many other things, their typical menu including the afore-mentioned earthworms, insects,

Foxes jump onto their prey, using their front paws.
This one is probably eating a beetle or earthworm.

Menu

(Top) Stag Beetle.
(Middle) One-day-old duckling.
(Bottom) Hedgehog recovering from a mite infestation.

(Top) Slug.
(Middle) Frog.
(Bottom) Various domestic fowl.

fruit and vegetables, berries, scavenged carrion and anything edible from domestic waste. Such luxuries as cakes, buns, jam, cheese and potatoes are also much appreciated.

Like cats and dogs, foxes eat grass. The purpose is unclear, but it may act as a source of roughage. The fox is again dog-like in its tendency to eat indigestible items that could perforate the stomach or intestine and kill the animal.

Foxes very rarely kill cats; cats form less than 1% of a fox's diet, and the cats taken are usually less than six months old or have already died as a result of a road accident. On the other hand, small pet animals and birds are at considerable risk if foxes inhabit the area and the owners do not secure their pets at night. Hutches must be bolted and the wire mesh on runs and aviaries must be secured both above and below ground, to save the occupants from being convenient take-aways for the hungry fox.

Feeding the Urban Fox

If you feed foxes regularly they will get into the habit of including you in their evening rounds. If you want to see them taking the food, put it out at the same time each evening. They soon become accustomed to garden lighting, and it ceases to bother them. Some become so tame that they will take food from your hands. I have never heard of a fox biting anyone who was feeding it, but hand-feeding should be avoided – a startled fox may snap.

Foxes sometimes stay and eat the food they find, but it is usually hidden in a cache, sometimes not completely buried. Occasionally a gardener may find chicken bones sticking up from a flower-bed. The buried food may be dug up by any member of the family group, as all will be familiar with family cache sites. They are not particularly fussy about how long the food has been left in their caches, but will dig it up and eat it many days after it has been buried.

Lawns sprinkled with bone or blood fertilisers are frequently excavated by eager foxes. The fox seems to be attracted by the smell of what it thinks is a buried dinner. It must be very frustrating for gardeners – and foxes!

Studying the Droppings

Fox droppings (scats) are a little smaller than dog droppings and are elongated and usually pointed at one end. They can be studied by scientists to find out what the foxes have been eating. The droppings are stored in individually labelled containers, soaked overnight and examined under a microscope for chaetae (earthworm hairs that look like needles). The faeces are then washed through a sieve until the water runs clear and then the debris is collected and examined under a microscope. Insect remains are identified by means of a suitable colour key, and the droppings will vary in colour according to what the fox has been eating.

I must emphasise that these are laboratory tests, and I am not recommending that the average garden naturalist should attempt them. In any case, droppings should never be handled without gloves.

Looking for dinner.

CHAPTER 4

The life of the FOX

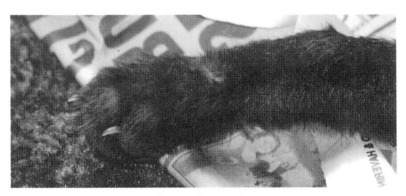

The paw of a young fox.

You will usually know when there are foxes about because, sooner or later, you will see them. However, you can also tell by droppings, hair and tracks. Droppings have already been described in the previous chapter, and fox hairs may be found near to pits and holes, between fence panelling and on barbed-wire fences. Their footprints are very distinctive, being made by the pads of the four toes, together with the central pad.

Family Groups

As has already been described in chapter 2, rural foxes tend to live and hunt in family groups. The dog fox, breeding vixen and cubs may be accompanied by one or more additional vixens. Usually they are all related, the adult non-breeding foxes being brothers and sisters of the mating pair or progeny from the previous year's

Paw prints (actual size).

litter. The non-mating foxes help to raise the family and the foxes usually become independent and disperse during the autumn, although quite often the whole family remain together for the winter. Such large family groups are uncommon in urban situations; foxes in urban areas have quite a high mortality rate, which does not allow for the build-up of such groups.

Territory and Range

Foxes are territorial animals, and they also have *home ranges* – areas in which family members will spend most of their time. A family of foxes will use a regular hunting pathway, which may include crawling under a particular piece of fencing and possibly going up to your back door. They may hunt right up to their territory boundary. The term *territory* refers to the area the fox will fight to defend and is usually smaller than and contained within the home range. Their territory can be looked upon as their 'home', their home range as their 'house and garden', and their den as their 'bedroom'.

Foxes spend a great deal of time foraging for food. The head is held close to the ground as it sniffs around.

Mating

Mating takes place in January and February. Cubs born early in the previous year will be ready to mate, and this is their pack dispersal period. At this time of year foxes are very vocal. The vixen is receptive for about three days and usually has only one mate. Copulation may take place at other times of the year but usually without the subsequent pregnancy, although vixens do sometimes have second litters during the summer months.

If the dog fox does not withdraw quickly from the mating he may lock inside the vixen for as much as an hour, as her vagina contracts and traps his penis. This is just like the 'tie' looked for in the mating of domestic dogs. The two animals end up facing back-to-back, and are obviously very vulnerable in this situation.

CHAPTER 4

A young fox in the nest.

Pregnancy and 'Nesting'

Pregnancy (gestation) lasts about 7½ weeks (52½ days). Vixens dig their 'nests' (called *earths* or *dens*) in February. Foxes are very adaptable, and the dens may be anywhere, but they particularly like them to be under sheds, extensions or thick hedges. They often dig tunnels to their dens, frequently having more than one entrance. In general, they will use any site they consider suitable and available, occupying deserted badger sets and even enlarging rabbit warrens to meet their needs.

Despite the fact that they prefer to be under flooring, foxes quite often breed above ground, raising their cubs in disused yards, amongst the rubbish. They have even been known to have their dens in attics! Occasionally, two related vixens and their litters may share a den, and two separate litters may sometimes live close together, having dens in the same garden or adjacent gardens.

Development of the Cubs

Two to six cubs are born around March. They are blind and deaf, but they do have some short, dark grey-black fur. At birth they weigh approximately 100g (3½oz).

The vixen does not leave the cubs to forage until about two weeks after the birth. She is fed by the dog fox during this period, the dog depositing the food in the den and retreating rapidly.

Two weeks At two weeks, the cubs' eyes open; the eyes are blue at this stage. Once the eyes are open the cubs can usually urinate on their own without being stimulated (having their genitals licked) by the mother. Their ears are typically rounded and they have short snouts. They start to bark at this age.

Three weeks The weaning process starts, the vixen giving the cubs regurgitated food.

This young fox is keeping an eye on its mother as it rests.

Four weeks The cubs begin to venture above ground. This is usually some time in April. The fur is now dark brown and the blue eyes are changing to yellow. They begin to eat solid food. In captivity cubs begin to eat puppy food. The adults begin to moult.

Five weeks The cubs start getting their adult colouring and shape. The short snout and ears elongate rapidly. The mother may begin to sleep away from the den to prevent the cubs from suckling.

Six weeks The cubs are playful and practise hunting. The black markings appear on the ears and legs, and the fur changes colour from sooty grey to lush red-brown.

Eight weeks The cubs are fully weaned and some may start to sleep away from the den, possibly above ground in thickets.

By the end of June all the cubs should be on solid food. The whole family may move above ground, into a nearby den, and less food is brought back for the family by the adult animals. In July the cubs start to move away from the den and hunt for themselves.

Dispersal

In September dispersal begins. By autumn the young foxes should be fully independent and ready for dispersal. However, sometimes the whole family stays together during the winter months. About one in four cubs will not survive the first four weeks of life, and by the autumn only about two thirds of them will be alive.

By October the adult moult has usually been completed. By December the juveniles will be fighting and establishing territories. At this time of year foxes are very active, preparing for the breeding season.

At dispersal the juveniles could move 100km or more. However, British urban foxes may only disperse over a range of 1–2km, and some may just move a few gardens away.

Prior to dispersal, some young foxes may make a number of exploratory tracks, possibly stopping away from home for one or more nights before returning. Then one day they will leave and not return again. Others will just get up and go, and yet others may go away for the winter and return to the home range for the spring.

The young foxes are at very high risk during dispersal and, by the following year, less than half the cubs born the previous year will be alive. In some urban areas, about 90% of the juveniles die within the first year of life.

Understanding the life of a fox helps us to understand and control the spread of disease. It also helps us to gain considerable pleasure from watching the urban fox. Foxes need cover – an undisturbed patch of brambles at the end of the garden would be suitable. Artificial dens can be built. The den needs to be about a metre (a yard) long and 30cm (a foot) high, with entrances made from drain pipes a metre long and 20cm (8in) in diameter. However, in urban situations, it would be unwise to encourage foxes too much (see chapter 8).

It is sometimes possible to determine the number of foxes in a given area by locating all the dens during April and May and then counting the number of cubs in each den. This is not easy. Firstly, you can never be sure that you have located all the dens in a given area, and some may be on private property. This would obviously be the case in cities and suburbs. Secondly, if a fox has four cubs, you could be counting the same cub twice unless you see them all together, because they all look very similar. Field workers generally resort to a mixture of methods including radio tracking, marking and tagging, counting dens and trap/release counts.

In the evening, foxes can often be seen from trains by commuters.

CHAPTER 5

Helping the sick FOX

A very sick fox being tended. Note that stout gloves are still necessary!

Many people like to help sick foxes. I receive numerous calls each year from distressed people with sick foxes in their gardens. The general rule is to leave well alone unless the fox is in a really critical condition.

There are several reasons for this seemingly heartless attitude. Firstly, if the fox is taken into care for any length of time, not only will it be very distressed but another fox will probably move into its territory. Consequently, when it is released it will no longer have a home, but will be regarded as an intruder and have a slim chance of survival.

Another point is that foxes and vixens taken into care from April to August may well have dependent cubs, who will then starve.

Yet another point is that, once a fox has been taken into care, it must be released back into a suitable location. With urban foxes, the wishes of residents must be considered and, with rural foxes, the wishes of farmers must be considered.

It follows that a fox must never be taken into care unless it is absolutely necessary. Veterinary treatment for foxes can be very expensive, and only the larger animal charities can cope with looking after them. In any case, a fox so badly hurt that it needs to be taken away is usually in such a bad condition that it will need to be destroyed humanely by a veterinary surgeon. If you want to help a sick fox, leave a shed door ajar and put out some food and water for it.

If the fox does have to be taken away, dog handling equipment will be needed. Otherwise, very thick gloves are a 'must', as injured and frightened foxes *will* bite. We generally use a trap for distressed foxes that need to be taken into care.

The sedative *Diazepam* has been used on foxes to allow full examinations to be carried out. However, the usual method is to anaesthetise the animal to allow safe and easy handling with minimal stress. Veterinary surgeons and large animal centres accustomed to handling wild patients may use crush cages. These have interior doors that can be moved inwards to trap the animal so that an injection can be administered safely.

Broken Bones and Dislocations

Many foxes survive broken bones in the wild – in fact, roughly a quarter of wild foxes have sustained a broken bone at one time or another. This is a surprisingly high figure, and shows that animals can overcome such injuries. Most limping foxes are best left well alone; they can usually cope, especially if someone feeds them and allows them access to shelter. Compound fractures, where the skin is broken and the bone can be seen, need veterinary attention, as do dislocations, where the limb is obviously out of place.

Arthritis

Arthritis is a common problem for foxes. As I have already said, limping foxes are best left alone, but given access to food and shelter. Arthritis is a progressive disease and animals taken into care and found to be suffering from it usually have to be humanely destroyed. This is because arthritis is incurable and painful and the animal's condition is likely to deteriorate with time. Its fate will depend on how ill it is but I must reiterate that, if a fox is sick enough to need to be taken into care, it is usually very sick indeed.

Poisons

Poisons such as insecticides and metals can accumulate in foxes. Foxes eat slugs and possibly also the poisonous slug pellets put down by gardeners. Affected animals appear tame and listless. In cases of acute poisoning, they may go into fits and show signs of distress. If they are well enough to be left in the garden, give them plenty of water to drink as well as food and shelter.

Infections

Foxes that have eaten unsuitable materials may end up with infections within their intestines or have membranes punctured by sharp objects.

Chest infections are common in foxes in the winter months, as they are in hedgehogs and humans. Bronchitis and pleurisy are often seen.

Diseases

Theoretically, foxes could contract canine distemper, parvovirus and hepatitis but cases involving foxes are very rare in Great Britain. However, they can contract leptospirosis (Weil's disease), against which pet dogs can be vaccinated. The causative organism is *Leptospira icterohaemorrhagiae* and it is passed through infected urine. Weil's disease is a worry when pet owners neglect to have their dogs vaccinated and allow them to foul public places, especially where children play. In foxes, this disease results in impaired function of the kidneys and it is sometimes seen in foxes that are more than a year old.

Very little work has been carried out on diseases that affect foxes and not people, but foxes can be vaccinated in the same manner as dogs.

Foxes and Rabies

Foxes are major carriers of rabies in mainland Europe. They are not the only carriers: humans, bats and domestic animals, especially pet dogs, are also instrumental in the spread of rabies. Nevertheless, the fox has been pinpointed as a major reservoir of rabies, and measures have been taken to reduce fox populations in areas where the disease is prevalent. The annual autumn dispersal patterns of the fox life cycle are a problem as young foxes leaving their home ranges can spread the disease further .

To put rabies into perspective, it should be remembered that, although it is a killer disease, modern control measures have ensured that very few people have died of it in recent times.

Previously, quarantine regulations ensured that all dogs entering Great Britain were kept for six months in secure, approved kennels, where they were monitored for symptoms of the disease. After this, if no symptoms were apparent, the pet was returned to its owner. In 2000, the Pet Travel Scheme (PETS) meant that cats and dogs could be taken abroad and back again without the need for quarantine. Further details, including a list of participating countries, are available from, PETS helpline Tel: 0870 241 1710 (9am-5pm week days) or Intervet UK Ltd, Walton Manor, Walton, Milton Keynes MK7 7AJ. Initial steps have been taken to replace quarantine with a vaccination policy, in which cats and dogs from European countries will be required to be vaccinated against rabies at least six months before entry into Great Britain.

Rabies is a real threat as it spreads across mainland Europe towards the ports. Furthermore, it is thought that the Channel Tunnel may pose an additional avenue of risk.

The spread of rabies among foxes has traditionally been controlled by killing any infected animals, by quarantine and by killing all foxes in affected areas. In such areas pet dogs are usually required to be muzzled. However, a new method of control is the immunisation of foxes by the use of bait doctored with an engineered live

A young fox that was brought to us in a box.

virus against rabies. Capsules containing the correct dosage are added to the bait, which is considerately more effective than the indiscriminate sprinkling of poison to kill the foxes. Altogether, immunisation seems a much more effective method of rabies control, and it is hoped that it will finally halt the spread of the disease across Europe.

Should they be unfortunate enough to catch rabies, pet dogs show marked behavioural changes in the advanced stages of the disease. There is a long incubation period, generally of about six months, but periods of up to a year have been recorded. Infected dogs become aggressive, and this is followed by fits. They may try to bite anything, including humans and other dogs, and will salivate copiously. Then there is progressive paralysis, followed by coma. One or all of these symptoms may be present before death.

If an animal is confirmed to be suffering from rabies, the disease is notified and the possibility of the animal having passed on the disease to others within the vicinity is considered. Rabies is spread by the bite of an infected animal, the virus entering the wound via the saliva.

Vaccination immediately after the bite helps to prevent the disease from developing – the longer the delay in being vaccinated, the more likely the disease is to develop. Once the symptoms are apparent, death is largely inevitable. Anyone bitten by an animal suspected of having rabies must be immunised immediately.

Parasites and the FOX

Parasites found on (external) and in (internal) healthy foxes are only a problem when the animal's resistance is low and the number of parasites increases excessively. They can be grouped as follows:

External parasites Mites, ticks, lice, fleas, flies.

Internal parasites Worms (including roundworms, tapeworms, flukes and spiny-headed worms) and other organisms.

External Parasites

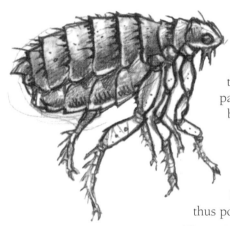

Flea.

External parasites are more common in the hot summer months, partly because warm weather conditions facilitate the breeding of parasites and partly because the nests of breeding vixens are a nice place for them to live in. It is particularly important to eradicate biting insects such as fleas and ticks because they bite one animal after another, thus potentially spreading disease.

Fleas Like pet dogs, foxes can and do become infested with fleas. Wild animals ensure that the parasite population is kept to a minimum by regular grooming, but ill health sometimes results in a flea problem. Also, when the youngsters are tiny they do not groom themselves very efficiently, and the den is used as a constant communal bed for a few months. These factors, combined with hot weather, could cause a build-up of fleas. Additionally, the den may become surrounded by bones and rotting pieces of meat brought there by the parents. Animals killed by the fox may

Tick.

also have had fleas, which have then been brought back on the carcass. All this can result in a flea problem.

During September 1997 a local primary school had to remain closed for a short time until the building was fumigated because of fleas. Foxes had made a den beneath the 'temporary' school building (erected during the 1950s!). It should be noted that such cases are rare.

Fortunately, the treatment is simple and effective. An insecticide spray for dogs rids a fox of its fleas. Foxes are usually treated for fleas on arrival at an animal sanctuary and, to ensure that the fleas do not become a problem, they and their bedding are treated regularly throughout their captivity. External parasite control should be a standard hygiene practice for companion and captive animals.

Ticks Surprisingly, many dog and cat owners do not know what ticks look like, although unfortunately they are plentiful. Anyone used to handling hedgehogs will be very familiar with these little beasts.

All animals can acquire ticks. They live in thick vegetation and crawl up animals' legs, remaining inconspicuous at first as they are only the size of a pin-head and are hidden in the animals' fur. They then proceed to bite and take a blood feed from their hosts, expanding to the size of a pea. This is when you notice them. Once the tick has become big, fat and well fed it may drop off the animal, living in the animal's bedding until it needs another feed.

Remove ticks by smothering them with cooking oil, surgical spirit, Vaseline or an insecticide spray for dogs. Wait about 15 minutes for them to die, and then remove them with tweezers. Be sure that the tick's head is removed, too, or it can cause infection. Fortunately, tick infestations in dogs and foxes are not common, but pet owners and wildlife sanctuaries should be aware that animals may acquire the odd tick.

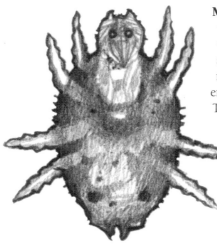

Mite.

Mites Mites that cause mange are particularly troublesome to foxes. *Otodectes cynotis* causes ear canker and *Sarcoptes scabiei* and *Noteodres* mites cause mange, which is endemic in many fox populations. This condition can be transmitted to dogs, but cats seem resistant. Handlers of foxes with mange are advised to take precautions.

Mites burrow into the skin and the fox loses weight and also much of its fur, which is replaced by crusts and scabs. Fox mange is largely due to *Sarcoptes scabiei*. The infection usually starts around the tail area, spreading to leave hairless patches of sore, crusty skin. Foxes can die from heavy infestations. It is highly contagious and, in the late stages, the animal may be in considerable distress. Affected foxes may attempt to hide away in garages and sheds because of their weakened condition and susceptibility to cold. In humans the disease is called *scabies*.

Thorough hygiene and dabbing with Benzyl Benzoate usually gets rid of scabies. Mange takes some time to show any signs of improvement, but it is treatable provided the animal has not been weakened by secondary infections as a result of wounds and sores. The veterinary surgeon may treat the conditions with injections, which are usually quite effective.

Internal Parasites

Foxes are susceptible to both roundworms and tapeworms. The common gut roundworm is *Toxocara canis*. Worms can sometimes be found in the bladder and lungs. Foxes can also carry heartworms, which can affect the lungs, liver and heart. Affected animals often cough and are usually underweight. The slug is the secondary host in the life cycle and the disease may be spread by foxes as they disperse.

Pet dogs need to be wormed regularly, as their close proximity to children and tendency to foul public places could put children at risk. By the same token, it is wise to worm captive foxes. Regular worming is standard practice for all pet owners and animal sanctuaries. Fortunately, it is simply a matter of giving the appropriate

"Ah, that's better!"

medication with food, and suitable tablets are usually available at veterinary practices and pet shops. The medication is relatively inexpensive and the treatment is usually very effective. It is wise to worm any animal that is any of the following: underweight, lethargic, coughing or wheezing.

CHAPTER 7

Feeding and releasing the FOX

The Adult Fox in Captivity

Only very rarely will an adult fox need to be kept captive. Such foxes eat any scraps and tinned dog and cat food. Sterilised bone meal can be added. They also eat dead day-old chicks and mice, which can be bought as food for snakes and hawks. Very heavy feed dishes are necessary or the fox will tip them over.

Finding Cubs

If you find a fox cub and are not sure whether to leave it alone – *please* leave it. Every year many cubs are taken into care unnecessarily. Animal hospitals and sanctuaries are publicised by the press as places offering a loving environment in which cubs will thrive. Consequently, many people are tempted to pick up a cub they see alone on a bleak spring morning and take it to one of these centres.

In nine out of ten cases, cubs need not be removed from where they are found. Vixens can sometimes locate lost cubs given time – in fact, cubs left behind in a move may be collected as late as the following night.

If adult foxes are not in evidence it does not automatically follow that the cubs have been abandoned. From June onwards, when the cubs are a couple of months old, the vixen may choose to sleep nearby, but in separate quarters. The dog fox does

Mushrooms for tea.

not normally sleep with the family at all, keeping a respectable distance even when bringing food.

Cubs in real distress are those that get lost and wander into dangerous places or situations and those so sick that they have been rejected. In addition, as there is a high mortality rate, there is a real possibility that both parents have been killed, leaving orphaned cubs. Cubs under six weeks old need to be given milk so, if the vixen is killed before the cubs are fully weaned, they will die if they are not bottle fed even if their father is around.

Each situation therefore has to be considered individually. If at all possible, leave a cub where it was found and watch it from a

"Shall we chase it? Will it taste good?"

distance. If it has not been collected by the following day, you could try again the next night. If by then it has still not been collected, unfortunately it will need to be taken into care.

How to Help

If one of the parents dies (which is quite common) the other may go on raising the cubs. If the lone parent cannot manage and the cubs are over six weeks old, food and water can be put out every night near the den to help them.

Although most people love to have foxes in their garden and help them, some will not put food out regularly for cubs and will turf out healthy families of foxes, hedgehogs, birds and anything else because they do not want them in their gardens. They telephone people like me and ask me to come and remove the evicted babies that are too young to run away. Even then, the mother may return to collect her babies once she has recovered from her initial fright.

Never put collars on cubs. Cubs are usually housed outdoors as they get older and escapees can suffer horrible deaths if their collars become restrictive and cut into the flesh or get caught on twigs or other obstacles.

Rearing Newborn Foxes

Newborn cubs need to be fed every two to three hours during the day and every three hours at night. Cubs like to feed all in one go – changing bottles half-way through a feed upsets them. It is better to increase the

If you are in any doubt whether a cub needs rescuing – please leave it.

bottle size according to their needs. They can be reared on formula milk designed for puppies, which is readily available from pet shops. Follow the instructions on the container just as you would for puppies.

The cubs should be fully weaned at eight weeks and, at twelve weeks, they should be eating all sorts of scraps. By this time you will need to house them in an outside pen. Remember that foxes can, and will, climb and dig, and any outside pen must accommodate these activities. The top must be enclosed with wire mesh and the wire mesh must extend below the ground. A tea-chest or rabbit hutch can serve as a shelter.

Releasing Adult Foxes

Foxes adapt readily to a captive life, but much has been written about the problems of tame foxes.

Adult foxes that have had to be taken captive can be released as soon as they have overcome their illnesses. A fox can manage with a missing back leg but one with a missing front leg is at a considerable disadvantage as it will have trouble digging and climbing.

Releasing Juveniles

Always remember that hand-reared cubs are much less certain to survive than those reared by their parents. This is largely because, when juveniles are released, they are encroaching on territory that has already been claimed. In addition to this, they will have to learn to find food and become accustomed to the environment without the protection of the vixen and dog fox. However, successful releases can be achieved if, from September, the foxes are released gradually from their compounds, the doors left open so that they can come and go as they wish. Food can be left daily until the fox does not return for food and shelter. Long-term adult casualties can be released in this way.

The urban fox sunning itself, but it always keeps a wary eye open.

Problems of the FOX

Most people seem to like having foxes around and have accepted urban foxes into their way of life, suffering their proximity. Nevertheless, there are people who find them a nuisance.

A Dangerous Animal?

As I have already recounted, in 1996 a fox is reported to have attacked a baby left in a pram in a conservatory. The baby's face was scratched, but it was otherwise unharmed. Though extremely upsetting, this report is exceptional – foxes are generally considered harmless.

Alleys and footpaths are often used as regular pathways by foxes on their nightly prowls.

Foxes and Gardeners

Most foxes can squeeze through gaps little more than 20cm (8in) square. There may be problems when they have dens under favourite flowering shrubs. They can also be smelly (fox urine is particularly offensive) and they sometimes chew through underground cables.

Most foxes are unobtrusive by nature, preferring to have their dens at a safe distance from their human neighbours – preferably under the garden shed or in some other quiet corner out of the way. However, playful cubs will certainly romp about in the garden, possibly flattening flowers and trampling through vegetable patches. They may also play in cloches and become entangled in pea netting. Small flower pots may be carried about and the odd shoe and fishbone may be found on the lawn. Food remnants may accumulate and start to smell if not cleared up, and stolen items from the washing line and playthings like balls and toys may find their way into the mouths of playful cubs. So be careful what you leave in your garden when foxes are around!

Foxes also eat fruit, especially soft fruit. However, it is usually the birds that get the blame!

Different people may complain about different aspects of a fox's life. To a gardener, digging up a flower bed may well be seen as a major crime, but to others different things can be equally annoying and lead to them persecuting the fox.

Noisy Neighbours

Foxes screaming in the night can be extremely disturbing. Usually this is a problem for only a couple of winter months, but litters of cubs also have their noisy moments.

Foxes and Livestock

Some people may be terrified that a fox will take their pet cat. On very rare occasions a weak kitten may be taken, but in general cats are much more at risk from humans, particularly from being run over.

Like many other carnivores, foxes are occasionally involved in overkill. A fox that gets into a chicken run may kill all the chickens there, while only eating one and taking away another to store in the cache. It kills because the chickens are readily available and it is natural for it to think of its food supply, even if it cannot carry them all away. Also, the chickens flutter about, which in turn panics the fox. The resulting pen full of dead birds is dreadfully upsetting to the chicken-keeper who discovers them in the morning.

Some distraught owners think they must kill the fox who raided the coop in case it returns again and again after its first taste of chicken. Unfortunately, all foxes within the area will be attracted to the chicken coop, and the onus is on the owner to ensure that *none* of them can get in. Rarely will an urban fox spend any length of time trying to get into a chicken run; it will usually get tired of looking and go after food that is more readily available. The fox is more persistent when it comes to deciding on the location of its den – which could well be under the chicken coop!

Foxes also take pet rabbits and guinea pigs if hutches are not bolted and runs are not completely surrounded by wire mesh. Until the wild rabbit population was

If you keep rabbits or guinea pigs in a run, make sure the top and base are secure.

drastically reduced by myxomatosis, these were a main prey of the fox, but afterwards the fox had to adapt to other food sources. Voles are another favourite, but they too are now becoming quite rare.

A fox will take a lamb, especially if it is weak and not guarded by its mother.

While cats and foxes do not often fight, pet dogs often chase foxes – in which case it is often the fox that gets bitten if caught.

Some people are afraid that a fox will mate their beloved pet dog. While dog foxes may show some interest in bitches, it would be virtually impossible for a successful breeding to occur because of the differences between the species. However, domestic dogs have often bred with wild canids that are more closely related, such as coyotes, wolves and jackals.

Scavengers

Foxes eat carrion. Often they are accused of killing animals when they have actually carried away an animal that has already died. Like cats and dogs, they often raid rubbish bins, especially if plastic bin bags are left lying around. It is very easy for the foxes to rip these open, so they should be stored in a garage or shed prior to collection day.

Foxes also eat food put out for the birds and can get through cat-flaps to eat the cat's dinner.

If foxes are around, aviaries should always be fox-proof, especially at ground level.

Controlling and hunting the FOX

Deterring Foxes

To stop foxes from foraging in your flower beds, try planting peppermint or garlic around the beds. To prevent them from using your garden in the first place, think about removing whatever is attracting them: for instance, the exposed plastic rubbish bins, the accessible hedgehog bowl or the low bird table. A two-metre fence will deter foxes from entering a garden, but they may well dig under the fence unless there is a concrete base.

Removing Foxes

If you want to get rid of a garden fox, translocation (removing the fox and releasing it elsewhere) is not the answer. Another fox will quickly move into any vacated territory. Furthermore, the fox that has lost its home will probably die, as it will be considered an intruder when released into another fox's territory. Also, urban foxes dumped in the countryside will not be used to the rural lifestyle. This should be remembered especially when you are rearing cubs, who really do need to be released slowly from a pen.

Be very careful if you need to get rid of a den. Remember that the fox may have cubs any time from March to August. If you disturb the den the foxes may move out anyway and any cubs will be carried away by the vixen. Remember also that the foxes may move out of the den of their own accord during August to September. If you need to know whether a den is being used leave a few sticks over the entrance(s).

If they are resistant and you really need to evict them, try using an animal repellent. Such repellents can be bought from pet stores, hardware shops and some veterinary practices.

Creosote will harm the fox's delicate feet, and will also affect cats and other pets. For this reason, it should not be spread around. However, a rag soaked in Creosote can be left in a closed container and pinned out of reach but near to the entrance of the den. This will cause the foxes to move home very quickly, and the den can then be filled in.

Fox Hunting

Hunting sports have always been associated with the nobility and are recorded way back into the Middle Ages. Fox hunting, deer hunting, big game hunting and grouse shooting were the sports of the rich. Poor people could not afford the time, the cost or the land for such hunting to take place, so contented themselves with such sports as falconry, fishing, ferreting, cock fighting and badger baiting. Fishing and ferreting for food have been accepted by most people in civilised societies.

Mounted hunters with packs of hounds have pursued a variety of quarry (the hunted animal) including foxes and deer. Fox hunting was extremely popular with the gentry during the 18th and 19th centuries. There may be about 30 hounds (hunting dogs) in a pack. Recognised hunts are protected from cruelty charges by clauses in the Animal Act. The main fox hunts take place in late autumn and winter, but cubbing (the practice of training young hounds by letting them catch and kill juvenile foxes) takes place from September to November.

Far from hunting to control the fox population, hunters often brought juvenile foxes into the area to keep the local population high. Indeed, it has been claimed that the popularity of fox hunting has helped to ensure that the Red Fox did not become extinct in Great Britain.

A home-made hedgehog nesting box. A small pipe will prevent a fox from disturbing the hedgehog and the container can be partly buried.

This type of trap can be used to catch a fox easily and safely – but only take a fox captive if it is absolutely necessary.

Fox Control

Nevertheless, gamekeepers and Scottish sheep farmers feel that some foxes must be killed to protect their stock, as foxes prey on game and weak newborn lambs. Foxes are often hunted on foot in Scotland, because of the rough terrain.

As about 50% of foxes in a given area die each year, control by killing would have little impact unless the kill were greater than the natural yearly mortality rate. Nature exists in a fine balance – if foxes were eliminated in a given area, the vole population, for example, might grow, along with the rabbit population and populations of vermin such as rats and mice.

In 1998 Professor S Harris of the University of Bristol released the report of a study confirming that the losses of lambs, piglets and poultry to foxes were insignificant compared to other forms of mortality. The report goes on to state that foxes can be beneficial to farmers by controlling rabbit populations.

Foxes have been controlled by the use of many different types of traps and by shooting, gassing and poisoning, as well as by hunting.

Gin traps were commonly used in Great Britain until banned from many areas during the 1950s. The gin trap is akin to an open jaw that closes when trodden on, holding the leg until the trapper returns to the trap.

Snares are commonly used in the form of steel wires that tighten around the animals' necks. Restricting snares, which continually tighten around the neck as the animal struggles, were made illegal in Great Britain in 1981, but free-running snares are legal. These are meant to trap the animal via the neck without strangling or throttling it as it struggles. Once a snare has been set, it is illegal to leave it for more than 24 hours to check whether an animal has been caught in it.

Shooting can cause suffering if the fox escapes with a bullet wound.

Gassing of fox earths with cyanide gas is another control method which has been used, but it was banned in Great Britain in 1981.

Poisoning has also been banned for controlling the fox population. It kills indiscriminately, affecting dogs, cats, badgers and hedgehogs as well as foxes. The other problem is getting the dosage right (see also chapter 5 under *Foxes and Rabies*). Poisons sprinkled onto bait are not suitable, as their effectiveness is dependent on the fox's hunger.

Hormones can also be applied to bait to sterilise foxes and thus control the population by preventing them from breeding. Again, it may also affect other species that eat the bait. Tests on a specially engineered virus are now being carried out, and it is hoped that the virus will target foxes and deliver the birth control hormone in this way. Tests so far indicate that this method may be both effective and safe. However, the possibility of environmental problems must be considered with the release of genetically engineered viruses.

Year in the life of the FOX

January	Mating takes place. Foxes are often heard calling.
February	The vixen chooses a suitable place in which to raise her young.
March	The cubs are born. The dog fox feeds the family while the vixen rests with the cubs.
April	The vixen starts to leave the den and feeds the family on regurgitated food. Vixens may fight neighbouring foxes at the boundaries of their territories.
May	The vixen and dog fox are busy bringing food to the den.
June	The cubs are frequently seen near the den. The adults often look scruffy as the moult progresses.
July	The cubs venture further afield and may 'lie up' overnight in undergrowth.
August	The cubs become independent.
September	Dispersal begins and juvenile foxes move away from the home range.
October	Foxes develop their winter coats.
November	Dispersal continues as foxes look for areas to sustain them through the winter months.
December	Dog foxes fight to defend their territories in preparation for mating.

Bibliography

Baines, C   *How to make a wildlife garden*   Elm Tree Books, 1985.

Bueler, L E   *Wild dogs of the world*   Constable, 1974.

Feltwell, J   *Discovering doorstep wildlife*   Hamlyn, 1985.

Harris, S   *Urban foxes*   Whittet Books Ltd, 1986.

Kolb, H   *Country foxes*   Whittet Books Ltd, 1996.

Lloyd, H G   *The red fox*   Batsford, 1980.

Useful Addresses

The Fox Project
The Old Chapel
Bradford Street
Tonbridge
Kent   TN9 1AW (Tel: 01732 367397)

Department of the Environment,
 Transport and the Regions
Tollgate House
Houlton Street
Bristol   BS2 9DJ (Tel: 01179 878000)

International Union for the Conservation of Nature
rue Mauverney 28
CH-1196 Gland
Switzerland

Ministry of Agriculture, Fisheries and Food (MAFF)
Whitehall Place
London   SW1A 2HD (Tel: 0207 273 3000)

Wildlife Trusts
The Kiln,
Waterside,
Mather Road,
Newark,
Notts   NG24 1WT (Tel: 01636 677711)

RSPCA
Causeway
Horsham
West Sussex   RH12 1HG (Tel: 01403 264181)
National Helpline (Tel: 0990 555999)

St Tiggywinkles
Wildlife Hospital Trust
Aston Road
Haddenham
Buckinghamshire   HP17 8AF (Tel: 01844 292292)

Index

Index